GLASS PSALMS

GLASS PSALMS

by
Jonathan Garfinkel

TURNSTONE PRESS

Turnstone Press
Artspace Building
607-100 Arthur Street
Winnipeg, MB
R3B 1H3 Canada
www.TurnstonePress.com

Turnstone Press gratefully acknowledges the assistance of The Canada Council for the Arts, the Manitoba Arts Council, the Government of Canada through the Book Publishing Industry Development Program and the Government of Manitoba through the Department of Culture, Heritage and Tourism, Arts Branch, for our publishing activities.

Cover design: Tétro Design
Interior design: Sharon Caseburg
Printed and bound in Canada by Kromar Printing Ltd. for Turnstone Press.

Library and Archives Canada Cataloguing in Publication

Garfinkel, Jonathan
  Glass psalms / Jonathan Garfinkel.

Poems.
ISBN 0-88801-309-4

  I. Title.

PS8563.A646G54 2005   C811'.6   C2005-901396-6

For my grandparents

Benjamin Bercovich
Jenny Cohen
Saul Garfinkel
Chasia-Leja Kaufman

Contents

When I was a child I sang in the synagogue choir,
I sang until my voice broke. I sang
first voice and second voice. I'll sing
until my heart breaks, first heart and second heart.
A psalm.

—Yehuda Amichai, *Psalm*

Longing on a large scale is what makes history.

—Don DeLillo, *Underworld*

GLASS PSALMS

I

THE NOMADIC ALTERNATIVE

I have proposed one title—'the nomadic alternative.'
We obviously won't use it. It is too rational a title for a subject that
appeals to irrational instincts.

—Bruce Chatwin, *Anatomy of Restlessness*

War

Come.
Let us be wars onto each other.
We will hide in our trenches,
duck under napalm, sing
reveille to the street
and the dusk.

In our silence we may eat
from each other's hands, the bones
of our foes. Do you hear
the madness of nations,
the master and slave
in this touch?

I have brought you diseases.
Taste my Sarajevos, my children,
the broken timber,
your hard charcoal hand.

Come close. Closer. Press your tongue
against the Cambodia of my arm,
taste the Hiroshima you have forgotten.

Undress, my love,
and show me Bergen-
Belsen. I will teach you
Mao-Tse-Tung.

Undress and be silent,
my love, hold still,
be still and be silent.

Mazra' eh al shrqya, West Bank

There is nothing special about this town.
The big boys hit the small boys
with sticks on their way home
from school. Workmen
slap the face of the village mongoloid.
The women bake bread in the oven's fire,
and their husbands eat it, laughing.

Graves mark the places
near the town square. Cardamon, bitter
coffee, talk of
visas to America or France.

There are no mortars or shells.
No five a.m. gunfire from the settlement
across the valley. There are the skilled
stonecutters, renovations for the rich,
those with money to dream of Palestine.

The Israeli military base
sits on the hilltop like an oversized helmet
housing a head too big for its own good,
and yet there is no ruining this town's normalcy.

The big continue to hit the small.
The village mongoloid tries to laugh
at the others' jokes.

A woman finishes baking for the day,
smears flour on her face,
so that even her tears
will soon turn to dough.

Qalandya Refugee Camp: Seven Scenes

*We travel in the chariots of the Psalms, sleep in the tents of the Prophets,
and are born again in the language of the Gypsies.*
                                        —Mahmoud Darwish, *We Travel Like All People*

Outside Damascus Gate: the Arab market. Secret
police interrogate a fig
merchant, exchange
bruises for fruit. Teenage boys burn
last year's models, a bonfire of
Vogue and *Elle* magazines climbing the stone wall.
Here's where I meet him,
Charlie, the old
Palestinian with throat cancer, cancer
of the leg, of the mouth.
I help him onto the bus to Ramallah. His breath smells
like yogurt past its expiry date, a thousand
tumours gone bad.

'Call me Charlie Chaplin.'
He gambles, carouses and laughs.
I offer him a cigarette. And the warm coals of our Cleopatras
gentle us for a moment.

At the checkpoint, the bus stops. Hours of traffic
asleep or growling.
Patience faints, cracks in the heat.

The whole lot for sale: chai, jeans, carburetors, prosthetic limbs.

'The whole holy shebang.'

I leave Charlie, coughing at the sun.
Walk into the West Bank.

~

The scene in Visconti's *Senso*, the Austrian soldier
confessing to his hopeful Venetian lover:
'It's so lonely being an occupying force.
People only want to get rid of you.
Nobody understands, nobody loves you.'

Yeah, well the fucker gets her anyway. Eventually she's moon-eyed,
dog-hungry for him. Throws him the entire
purse of the Italian revolution
so he can wait for her in Verona. Passion,
that miserable sow, wins again.

At the end of the war
she travels hundreds of miles for him.
Past a handless soldier trying to eat
lentil soup, civilized. Past farms and women
lying bruised and empty. Until she finds him
drunk in Verona, his head
trapped in another pussy—

another
        'unwanted situation.'

The soldiers at this checkpoint: faces,
like any faces. Brothers, like any.

No romance here.

~

All of this is beside the point. A waterfall of rebar
flows from blown-out buildings they call homes.
And the children's games:
                              pelt each other
hard as they can, often as they can—
rotten fruit, flat batteries of stone,
carcasses of car parts.

                         Anything

to avoid what is in
or what is missing in them.

Aching to play, to maim.

~

This is where we smoke in secret.
This is where we take the girls
and learn what we don't know
how to do yet.

We're good friends. At night we pray, smoke,
rub our bodies against stone. Anything
to create a spark.

Over here: windows checkered with bullets from the IDF.
And there: fruit straight from the tree, hard and bitter to eat.
And here: sweet coffee and cardamon. Old men
playing *shesh besh*. Game of the damned.

We go to school when we can.
Learn history, geography
if there are books.
Come home to the smell of mint and sage tea.

His grandmother smells like cardamon and shit,
but that all started when the missiles
landed on the cowshed. You should've seen the way cows'
heads split open. Blood and brains
rained over the valley. It was biblical,
manna, everything purple. Some say Crazy Boy
ate the leftovers. That's why he's crazy they say.

We won't be stupid like Crazy Boy. See him? He's the guy
collecting stones. Gonna bring them
to the checkpoint. For every seven of us,
there's one who goes crazy. We won't. We still cry
when we visit our friend's grave. We're afraid
when we hear helicopters in the night, sound of
wound-up ducks, sprung on you
in no time.

Don't mind the gunfire.
Crazy Boy started throwing stones again.
His stones don't forget.
Blood on the tongue,
fire in the head.
A rubber bullet can be a good thing.

~

At the UNRWA daycare centre I'm surrounded.
We draw pictures, me and dozens
of children: butterflies take flight,
their wings turn to ash, sulphuring
the meadows. Cockroaches
leap through hoops of fire,
emerge strangely intact. Smoke and sirens
irritate the alley two streets over.

Marriage proposals die in the air.
Everyone wants their pictures taken, their souls possessed.
The kids adopt their favourite poses: J-Lo,
Madonna, Spiderman, the Sphinx.

For one afternoon, we are Hollywood.

~

   Greeted by
                    gunfire I leap
            three feet
                             in the air

   everyone else walks on
                    this is normal why
                         should
                                   things be otherwise?

            The army jeep
                                        100
   metres away   leers from
   the top of the hill

                                        (Crazy Boy out there w/
                            his collection of stones makes the most
                                of the afternoon   nobody concerned)

                                        (I'm given
                                    orange crush
                        by one of the boys   meant to keep me calm)

              Sam
speaks
good English,
his bonfire

                    courting

                                    the electrical fence. He burns
whatever people offer,
                        keeps the pocked area of road in order.
            Picks up an Arabic

                            Western Union ad: 'Bring this
to the people of
            Canada, show them what
we're enduring.'

                                        More gun-fff-
                    ire. Three soldiers kneel,
            bullets
                    spl-
ash
            us. On the radio, an ad for King Falafel:

                                        12

Our balls are the best
in all of Ramallah!   The details

addle, nothing told
.   straight.

                'I talk about wheat in my sleep,' Sam explains.
        A child without a shoulder
                    walks toward me. His mother holds the wound.
        Things don't hold together the way they should.

        Jeep approaches.
Sam's
        words, the gasoline

        in his mouth,
garbage in the fire, my warm
orange crush

        (At this very moment in Ramallah someone stuffs his
        face with eggplant and pita, hummus dripping
        on his hand. Pity and rubber bullets through our hands.
        Ingredients of confusion. In Canada my brother races
        early morning to work, Bloor subway, signs subliminal
        clanking *Castle Frank Broadview Pape*). Sam

stuffs the ad down my pants. 'Don't forget,' he says.

        And I'm gone. Pass-
port, metal detector, check-
point. Back
to the other side.

            My heart is limping.

~

Pull over a car.
Driver I have only three
dollars. Where can you take me?

Leaves me at Mea She'arim. The alleys. Almost evening:
the night before Passover.
Jews burn *chametz*, sweet bread,
to mark the water-and-desert
passage from slavery.

Men scurry to the ovens before dark. Everywhere,
the music of people, burnt
bread and prayers.

On an empty street, a boy of eight assails me,
throws stones at my camera.

'Go,' he says.

'Go where?' I ask.

And he runs too.

For a moment, there is silence.
A curtain of laundry, whites only, hangs,
bleaching in sun.

Prayer of the West Bank Falafel Merchant

Brother, the hummus is fresh. I ground the chickpeas
myself. I swear. By my life. It's good, fair price.

Do I look like I do this for fun? We're talking business. An eye
for an eye. Food for food.

Trust me, brother. There's nothing wrong
with it. I made this meal with my hands. Shaped
the earth, raised Abel from the dead. What more can a man do?

Name your price. Come on, brother! The food has to
be eaten. Give me something. A shekel. A seed. The sharp
edge of your knife. It will be our bond.
Our seal. Fair price.

Blood
and the taste
of your neighbours.

Turkish Bath

…This is the truth. This is not a dream brought back from another world past the customs officer, like a teapot from Mecca. I heard the water, and I was afraid.
—Paul Bowles

I wish I could say they're beautiful,
their faces like the light from the Blue Mosque,
soft on the eyes, supple in the head.
But no: they're fat and old.
They fart and laugh,
stare and ask, why don't I
join them?

I wash my feet. They smoke, the air
nicotine and sulphur. Then they pull on
each other, their silence
betrayed only by breath. A hand job
can be like this between men: where the real
devotion begins.

Their bodies rev until they stall, breath
stopped at the brink. They almost
come at the same time. I try
to speak, dodge the look,
say something casual, nothing
comes out. The towel boy
sings, washes the aged marble
with his white towel and black plastic
bucket. Cigarettes turn red
from their breathing. Pearls of hot water
fall from the domed, transparent ceiling.
Shadows of larks loiter above,
praising the day.

The Shoichet's Room

First time in Warsaw step off the Midnight
no money and the worst
snowstorm in 17 years. Two kids from the polytech school
take pity let me crash on their
mock marble floor, drink Zywiec and watch
Dirty Dancing dubbed in Polish. One man, one monotonous voice.
He gives Patrick Swayze a little more
crotch in the vowels, you can tell he
wants to be Swayze.
Easy.

Next day I visit the synagogue, a survivor
renovated by a cosmetics company.
They give me the room of the shoichet. It's free and overlooks
the frozen street, frozen time.
The shoichet, out of town for the weekend, killing
veal and chicken in Hungary.
God protects me in Poland. I believe.

The room's cold, without ornaments.
No pictures of family, favourite sheep or
ancestors. A book of
Stanislawksi, open: *the body is the tower
and the voice.* Heat vents exhale
herring and onions. A small single bed gulps
December's white light. One imagines
the gastronomic body
of Lazar in *Fiddler on the Roof.* The bed
can fit half a Lazar, no more.

I listen for ghosts, signs,
something of the past, hear nothing
but nine men in search of a minyan, voices
limping two stories below. I join them,
and we lamely
welcome the Sabbath bride. When the prayers are over,
there's vodka and wine by the caseload.
A different prayer, familiar.

There's Ruben who didn't know he was a Jew until twenty-one.
And Piotr who converted because the meals were free on Saturdays.
The other seven, old and dying.
Memory eclipsed, prayers forgotten.

Mickey the security guard won't pray at all.
His story: escaped Majdanek, joined the Partisans,
caught, then sent to Auschwitz. Under the red
moon he ran away with a circus
on a train to Shanghai. When he watched his father
chowed down by Japanese dogs
he could juggle balls, six at once. Now he eats
pickled eggs, belches,
won't pray to a soul.

Back in the room, I find a tape—
Leonard Cohen in the top drawer of the desk:
Is this what you wanted
to live in a house that is haunted . . .
Nothing to do but drink and pray.
Wonder about Mickey's fate.
Start to dance by myself, in front of the mirror.
Feel sexy, in spite of myself.
Alive, in spite of Warsaw.

Funny how these things happen.
The razed ghetto walls,
an entire city razed.
And all that was old
Warsaw now rebuilt
the memories of its citizens
lifting it up
stone for stone.

Snow falls until you're not sure if the world
exists. I feel not myself
and myself at the same time,
lost and not yet discovered,
much like Warsaw, much like this
half-Lazar of a shoichet,
when he slides his blade across an animal's neck
and feels its voice, hot in his hands.

On the Way to Jedwabne

The highways to Zakopane were flooded, and besides,
there was the memorial in the newspapers everyone talked about,
place-to-be, event-of-the-year, Soho-of-
Eastern Europe. I confess all I saw were your thighs
as we drove north and east out of Warsaw. We stopped and pissed
on the stones of Treblinka, drank Zubrowka, ate perogi,
saluted the Village of the Dead.

There was something chasing us, the Clash on the radio or 18-
wheel trucks cleaving the centre of the road, two lanes
gashed into three. We passed through
night-towns, like overworked students
skimmed our eyes over the memorials,
names: *Kielce, Lublin, Lodz.*

Past Bialystok a Turkish hotel near the border
lobby decorated with plastic cypress and recorded crickets,
looped for eternity. A stuffed boar
at the elevator. Its fake whiskered welcome.

Upstairs the street light
surprised us. The drunk in the alley
sang a song of longing for Lithuania. The white room,
my Jewish knees, your Polish-Catholic heat.

I became your textbook. So many ways
to read with lips. You demanded
my chest be glass, wanted to see
the whole sacred history:
capillaries, liver toxin, the ancient
whatever buried beneath.

Afterward, we could hear the news
in the room beside us. Images reeled. Tomorrow's memorial
had already begun: sixty years passed
since sixteen-hundred
blazed in that barn.

Only the crickets still sing.
A dirge.

Babyn Yar

The television spoke.
I saw my life, the shame like a newsflash,
broadcast across Kyev.

I built my memorial from bramble. Broken
tires. Heat lightning and glass.
David's pipe burned, then rested.
Dandelions turned from yellow to white,
children blowing the dead
weeds like smoke.

The earth so soft, I could not wake.
The tower saw this too.

                          Saw me.
Fallen asleep in Babyn Yar.

Layover

In the overnight lounge, I found myself
in the arms of a woman from Berlin. She was
writing her PhD in Logic, and I
was lost in her left elbow. I crevassed my head
into the space between her arm and chest.
And my right hand descended
into her heat.

I slept. Dreamt. Dogs
and church bells
chased me. Subways
offended the dead
rats, old bones. Night-watchmen
smoked, sang hymns
to the swallows. The streets of Berlin
undressed: red, damp,
full of pity.

II

PSALMS THAT WON'T
CHANGE THE WORLD

*I bent till my lips touched her ear
And whispered, 'I'll tell you, Lena,
Actually, I thought it up myself.
And there's no better song in the world.'*

—Anna Akhmatova, *By the Seashore*

Childhood

There was no blood on the silver
aspen. No trenches
beneath lupine, no brooks
trembling with contaminated fish,
polluted memory.

There were Mercedes, cool
as morphine. Gucci leather shoes
on the Day of Atonement. *Bonbons*
and Valium, stacked
high in the bowls of the neighbourhood moms.

There were no monsters in the moat,
no Mengeles beneath the bed.
The only doctors I knew were sweet,
and prayed sweetly too.
Their hot-chocolate voices
thick in their throats.

My mother, bless her still-rough, Salter Street
hands, taught me Chopin and Bach.

On a fall day, the sun would set, sleek, a ribbon
in the west. And the plush
white carpet of the living room
would betray itself, blushing,
as though embarrassed by
all this beauty.

Day of Atonement (Yom Kippur):
A Diabetic's Notebook, Kensington Market

Daffodils
fall away from each other
underneath the rain.

A pair of shoes
tied to telephone wires.

Wind walks the sky.

My grey veins, the window's
bent light.

Shadows clasp this
room, preventing
furniture.

~

Now I bow, smell of
curry in my hair

Cut garlic
Press lime

Pour rancid wine
into a yellow bowl

My dead pancreas
won't allow me this fast

~

Father

In the Minsker synagogue, we stand
side by side, prayer to prayer. I bow.
Your beard accidentally
brushes my forehead. I keep waiting
for your kiss. The rabbi
speaks of forgiveness between men.
You and I say nothing. Regret nothing.
The 24-hour Dim Sum sign
tempts pink across St. Andrew.
Eat. And you shall be satiated.

On the next page of prayer, we will confess
all of our sins.

Clenched hearts;
beating fists . . .

~

On Rosh Hashonah it is written

The universe
a Gothic Romance
God carries around
in Her pocket.

God the novelist,
ventriloquist and invisible
comic. We
the ink,
slip carefully
toward the page . . .

~

In near darkness, I inject
insulin into my abdomen. Shadows
lily the page. The Beatles
LP crackles and skips—

I'm fixing a hole
I'm fixing a hole

Rain leafs through eavestroughs.

Bicycles slick on asphalt.

Potholes
filled and forgotten—
like healed-over graves.

~

By Al Waxman Statue
for Dov M.

During the afternoon break, rains stop and we
sit by Al Waxman Statue. Consider
an appropriate word, gesture,
offering. While so-and-so devours
a mess of pastrami,
leaves half on the wet bench
next to my thigh.

The golden temptation, call it mustard,
spread like a vision across rye bread.
The hot meat, cold smoked,
siesta of raw coleslaw and onion.

A pigeon lands on Al's head. A river of white
gurgles from his ear, down his chest—
the shit-splayed stomach.
All in good taste.

Children vie for their place in the playground,
pummel each other one moment,
embrace the next.
                        Relentless.
Slapstick.

~

Listen: I crawl before You.

Can You hear my dry elbows
mulch green carpet? See how I
grovel to scratch
the poison ivy from my head?

I have left everything.
The garden, hell,
the beekeeper's daughter.

My heart, old compass,
mast burning at sea.

~

But of your kneecaps and
                              thighs:

what higher thoughts
can a man have?

~

Sandy Koufax was a helluva
Jew. You should've seen the way
he held his prayer book, south paw,
fingers split on the binding
as though he were gonna pitch God
out and away from the
plate.

When Koufax bowed before the beemah,
women from the gallery
grew moist from thigh to neck.
When Koufax chanted, men
sang harder, higher.
And their hopes did too.

In the heat of the Pennant,
in the hurricane of fast cars, slim
shiksas, Koufax fasted.
Brooklyn gasped. Doctors
swayed. And the earth beneath
the synagogue rose to its feet.

~

How does the diabetic fast on Yom Kippur?

He grinds his prayers into salt.
He lusts after candy
in the mouths of small children.

A rusted engine in an abandoned alley,
he sits alone with himself. The cleanse
begins with cutting onions. His tears
fall into the meal he prepares.

When he eats
he eats a part of himself,
broken off, afraid,
transformed into something
greater, and something less
than what once he was.

~

Do You like
spiral notebooks,
pages without lines,
premium, recycled paper?

Even toilet paper
for honest prayers?

~

Dear Rick Salutin,

Spadina may have gone hot and sour,
but I'm davening with the old guys
at the Minsk. Pesach's shirt
is stained red from
God-knows-what, and Morris
has fallen asleep again, a truah of snores
to replace the traditional
shofar blow.

In Forest Hill, red flags bartered
for five-dollar lattes. Seamstresses' hands
gone soft and fat
like a rash of Italian bacon.
At Holy Blossom, a psychiatrist paid $5000
for the final aliyah
before the gates of heaven close.
Money to Israel
plant a tree or a grave.

So sayeth the Lord:

Downtown shall move uptown. Factories
will turn into lofts. The rich will pray,
the poor will pay. And none of these debts
forgiven.

~

In this book, lists.
Pros and cons and
possible life choices.
Toothpaste smeared
on the cover, dried
from the last trip. Horrible
love poems to nobody.

Boredom, mostly.

~

I'm reading the prayer book
as if it's the story of our last year.

The confused heart.
The eye-bright glance.
The unholy, holy thoughts.

Close-up, interior of a scarred synagogue:
a lion on the wall, sleeping. A cedar
guitar and Belorussian clarinet, painted.
The red and glass
domed ceiling. Heaven. Rows of
pink and white blouses.

There you are. Blue eyes
hidden
behind a prayer.

How time courts the ancient.
And the memory of skin
grafts this distance.

~

Hypoglycemia

After 5 minutes: The body turns to honey.
                          Flies gather to lick the lips.

After 15:   Lack of glucose and oxygen to the brain.

After 30:   Candy-cane cocktails. The sticky red light.

After 60:   The moment before coma.
                          If you can, decide:

                          Candy floss, or earth.

~

On Yom Kippur It Is Sealed

The sound between beats.
The talk among beasts.
The distance between stars.
The home
that shakes in the wind.
The prayer
drowned in soil.

The leaf
gold
then brown
then nothing
and the white
everywhere

Zaida's Razor

Found Zaida's razor in a case of Campbell tomato soup, one of
thirty-three cases he bought the week before he died.

My grandfather was preparing for Apocalypse,
the thermonuclear,
the day sky would smash in light.
Soup to warm the belly. Razor to mollify the wrist.

Outside, the market. Credit cards. Fish.
Announcement: we are new flint
struck against stone.

I'm laying down the tracks of my desire.
And my cry: grate and spark of streetcars,
heavy metal traffic.

What is hidden
inside the *mezzuzah*. The electric
Spadina heart.

Advice from Zagajewski

You are thinking too much
about history and war.
Too much memory
ballasting the light.

Try music. Words you've never
heard. The wind
at point-blank. A new
language to kite the mind.

Try baseball. A fly ball
lost in the lights. White planets
gulped whole by the sky. Try
adultery. Balloons.
A piercing on a body part
you forgot you had. Anything
to puncture your throat.

Try the everyday. A doctor's
stethoscope. Smell of
coffee before it's swallowed.
Wet ink or a dry page.
Bridges, or mint.

Try turning on the light,
and listening to its patience.

The Night I Left

It was the first night I heard
the tree-frogs. Their song,
my family sleeping, the voices
stars in my skin.

And then the fireflies over our field.
The rockets in my ears.

Walking into darkness.
Feeling my wings.

Alone in a Room: a Still Life

A young man slouches at an apricot desk. Behind him
incense curls like a highway, destination and origin
unknown. Newspapers
thick with black and white regrets
litter the floor of this
landscape.

Beside him the bed that houses his life:
crumpled sweaters, tired paper,
warm evidence of a man
who reads, sleeps, and dreams.

On the desk, a book by Primo Levi, breathing.
Perhaps the phone rings, reminds the man
he knows nothing
about that place where poetry
was led to its hot death.

In this still life, the sun
always setting. Five-hundred-year-old chants
fill the rim of the room. A stereo plays hymns,
computers sound like heaven.
The glass of the window expands, grinning.

The young man has entered his purgatory with the greatest patience.
Old monk he has abandoned
everything for this moment.
Peace for a pen.
Silence for music. His eyes
for winter's frail light.

Testament

Genesis

At first I didn't understand. I was born. I hungered
until I heard myself. The world read me.

So my body named, divided
night from day,
woman from man, the waters
split in two.

                                  A page. A day.
A chapter.
One week.

My skin like a prophecy
bulged
from the earth.

~

Beginnings

The first ones had it good. I gave them a garden, innocence,
one language. You should've heard the music
among frogs and cranes, the lush
choral sound, grassy
echo of the beasts. Angels were
my secretaries, hard at work
among the eucalyptus, but joyous.

Even the garden became over-
canopied, blossom-heavy. There was no fall
as you'd prefer to think: Adam and Eve
simply could not find the door.

I loved Noah, he was my hope.
But I loved the Tower even more. Awesome
is the arrogance of men. Blessed
is their delusion, their faith
in ideas and bricks.

With lightning bolts
and darkness, I laughed at them.
Laughed so hard, I smashed
their language. How beautiful
the destruction! What colours
in this light!

A thousand dialects. The world's larynx,
squashed open across the floor.

Too early, the earth became hoarse with loathing.

~

Noah

When he can't sleep
I see him with his left ear
pressed to the pine deck.

He listens for knots
in the wood

~

Abraham

Now I can get down to the right
sound of myself. These are good
days. A man who listens. It's only now
I realize how lonely my words have been.

I inscribe secrets. New idioms
that curtain the air. For each sentence he reads,
a newer one revealed. I test him
in riddles: *Where are you?*
I am here. He ascends mountains,
prepares an impossible sacrifice. I'm demanding, jealous—
but who can blame me, a world
so unfaithful?

Yet he follows, and listens. Follows the first
sounds of alarm in the ram.
That's what wins my trust.
We compose our pact in the stars. I promise
offspring. He offers his body. I stitch
the borders of his home with my right hand,
and with my left—
                        I keep him close.

In the end, he's no different
from any of you:
a child, afraid of the night,
listening to the stories of his father.

~

Joseph's Prayer

Joseph, you arrogant prick,
                          I like you
where you are, brotherless, jammed
down a hole without water or hope. You'll learn fast: light
is the icing of the universe. See too much, you think
only of the surface, your *la-de-da* coat,
the swollen, hyperglycemic skin.

Of course I hear you. But it's more than an ear
you cry for. It's a hand you need, a step up,
a path through the crammed and doorless world.

Your prayers
dank books
tacked down
by the earth's light.

I hear you, feet quiet as loam.

Remember the blind
man. Be faithful
to the earth-
worm. To your voice
crumpled beneath shadow.

~

Exodus

To write something, there must be twists along the way.
The unexpected is law. Irony leads me
in its pillar of fire. Mysticism a cloud of smoke.

Screw the lessons behind the stories.
What I really want is a lasting entertainment.

I tell you: I wanted to create a miracle of literature. To burn
without burning, to write
without compromise. Novels of
frogs, leaping from the darkness. Epics of
boils, an erupting alchemy.
Contradictions, characters who could change
hearts on a dime. I developed structure. Control. Mastery:
                                        slew only the first born.

For forty years, they wandered the desert. Sand
stinging their faces. My words,
twisting suns, exacting sweat.
Stone for their faithlessness.

Bronzed, wind-thrown, I excavated their desire.

Brought them to their home.

~

Korach

Korach, you were the first Communist,
I'll give you that. In the desert you
raised your voice red like a flag,
and with your good looks and Trotsky hair
you led the masses against Moses,
against my word. Saying:
Kill the priests. Open the vault.
Let us all sing, o nation of prophets.

Then the earth opened, and swallowed
you whole.

The last word.

~

The Legend of David and the Foreskins

That's the one thing David had in common with Eichmann,
I always said. He knew you get more done
with a sword than a prayer. Later there'd be suckers
like Akiva, hippies like Nachman. Only David understood
the wisdom of the blade.

Goliath lay there in his blood and arrogance. Israel
slew the Philistines beautifully. David
took a dagger and removed
the foreskins of two hundred fresh dead. Perfect.

'Inspiration?' I asked him.
'God,' he replied.

I swear on my word
they were still warm from breathing.

~

Confession

The universe is chock full of disaster. I spend my days
editing. Frugal. No time to write
the new; it's all variations on a theme, fugue, endless replay.

There are structural problems in the outer dimensions. Loose pages
in unspeakable realms. Sometimes time
stops and I can't remember
the last sentence I wrote. *Oy.*
Sunspots, black holes, comets
shivering to no particular end:
these days, the heavens demand such complications.

What remains are the little miracles, the day-to-day.
It is the new Bible we write: moments to tie on a string.
Wear like an opal necklace.

Wind. Glass. Mint.

~

Rebuilding the Temple

Walk through the dark field.
Owl cry before flight.

Crowded by trees.

Their branches
bowing before me.

III

RUNNING INTO FIRE

Love, the real,
terrifies
the dreamer in his riot cell.

—Michael Ondaatje, *Gold and Black*

Manitoulin Ferry
for Robert Kroetsch and Paul Thompson

and

I would love
to fall again, to stumble,
let out that
fumbled cry, my fingers
            blind or dumb

but

it's like riding a bicycle

and

the woman in green
watches my nipples, I can tell she's
started reading her mystery
upside down

but

the sun is more of the man,
my eyes wobble when I think,
at least that's what I hear

and

I eat my carrot, the deckman
sprays cold water across the lower deck

but

the heat of day does not
listen to the hard spray of raw hoses

and

they say diamonds appear
in the most unlikely of places

but

that never seems to happen
when I want it to

and

I will eat another carrot

but

I wear chains around my ankles
at least that's what my therapist says
when I stand on the leather couch
explaining to her flight
is a state of mind

and

thank God I'm not married

but

I miss traveling close to water,
that sailing toward something
more, perfect union, man,
mast, sea

and

it is the sea that carries the line

but

Hemingway shot his swollen head anyway

and

I'm still not married

but

the waves come faster, I hear voices
sun's echo between my ears

and

a cavern opens beneath the boat,
the hull's heavy breath,
the lumbering channel

but

I sit on the deck of this 300-car ferry

and

the ferry will reach the shore

but

I follow the woman in green
sweater to the bow of the ship
she reads her mystery
leans on a long white post

and

the wind pushes her
she moves to turn the page
for a moment the sky speaks
as if somebody watches

My Desire Is Kansas

My desire is Kansas.
The sonar pitch of cornfields
ejaculating into the sour mash sky.

I like my wine, and I like my friends,
and I like my friends with wine.

But I desire you,
frail as heron-bone,
fancy as the prairies' clouds after thunder.

My desire is Midwest, is motorcycle,
teeth and zippers that burn
100 miles in the dark.

I like my friends, their blues and burnt bridges,
their civil war and ascension.

But I desire you.

First Touch

After we finish pulling scarlet
paintbrush and sage
from the fields, and you teach me
how to make music in my hands with
the tall grass, and we name all
the horses and cats on the farm,
I pull you towards me.
Our bodies become the first light
they click on in the barn.

Farm shadows fail
before our light.

Season

Now the farmhouse shakes
when a Ford blows by,
and gravel marks its feet.
Gone is the hare. The road abandoned
for forest, stone for spring.

The wallpaper breathes
in the upstairs room,
and the Chinatown lantern sleeps.
The bed, covered in ash,
starts to stir.

From the ash four hands are born,
and they sift through cinders and dust.
Two torsoes, coiled as heat.
And the wallpaper isn't sure
if it hears wind or love.

Now the golden bed trembles.
And flames begin to climb.
And the hands make twenty promises,
before they fall to heat.

Outside, a song of chrome and rust
returns the sun to ash, hands to earth.
And the wound
fills with darkness.

The Cat Was Bored

The cat was bored.
Through the window, he could make out
a single claw of paper, pawing the sky.
A pigeon braced itself
against the air, messageless.
You and I in love again,
above the bakery,
above the heat.

Thankfully, there was no conversation.
Our thoughts, like our bodies, had left us.
Our arms, warm and weightless
like newly baked bread.
On the radio, a gypsy song:
We are still here, though we are broken.

The story is us, and that room.
The story is the white sheets, summer fan,
and the cat, always watching.

Older than heat, the cracks of those walls.
Everything listens.
Everything waits.

So does our love.

Bathtub

Last night I traveled
all sails set to Jerusalem.

In the coral waves,
a moon sent me
east
on her sea.

I drank to the night,
and doves flew
toward my empty cup.

When the desert sweat fell from me,
I became the space, sun,
six vultures
circling my brow.

I have lived my life
in large rooms. This
is the only freedom
I ask of you.

One Word

You insisted on doing this
without Valium. I walked
into the room with you,
watched as you changed into blue
hospital pyjamas. Your belly,
not yet swollen.

I held your right hand. You lay back,
feet in beige stirrups.
The doctor emerged,
covering her yellow tulip skirt
in a blue uniform.

She put a tube inside you,
turned a machine on
and you screamed. I saw
blood and fetus
travel through the tube.

What did you say? My hand
on your forehead, became
your forehead, your witness,
your sweat. The doctor
said keep your legs
apart. You screamed. Again.
No words. I am sure.

Blood to the box,
metal beige box. Cold
to the skin, clots and tissue
and fetus caught in the filter. You screamed.
My hand in yours. Yours in mine.

The machine died with a groan.
The door swallowing
the doctor's faint yellow skirt.

Finally. The white
walls, your sore belly.
Your eyes
fluorescent and trembling. The sound
of your chest
fighting its breath. Only you
me saying

okay   okay   okay

and the walls
that knew nothing.

Shabbos   (Sabbath)
for Jennifer

Maariv (evening prayer)

The world weeps. Hours
measured by incense. Slow
spirals of skin.

We are the high
priests. Fingernails
on white pages, psalms
written on snow.

In the temple, a sky of black silk.

To light the eyes,
to pave the room with gold.

When we undress in darkness,
when we hold and
tear and send out voices, hurtling
to meet the night . . .

Bring me your offerings. The living
for the dead.

And I will call this barter
happiness.

~

Ritual

I have slain the wild bull.
Burned its black skin.
I have brought you ashes. Blood
dark with sand. Miracle
of glass. Molten prayers
for your golden sheath.

And on the blade we see the lovers,
their embrace bold as

               smoke

~

shekhinah speaks   *(sabbath goddess)*

goddamn these
prayers i'm so

hungry and the night

full of streetcars
as a child i used to wear

72 ornaments (bells and

pomegranates on my hips)
people used to know me by sound

when i walked the earth

spoke through the cracks of
torn pavement

kadosh kadosh kadosh

the yellow bags of garbage
screaming their obscenities

~

What I Want

I want this silence to spread its hands like a desert.
I want to bury my body
in the palms of sunlight, my lion
star melting in the alley's grey wrist.

I want Toronto to learn this hunger:
how a woman and man can knead
their bodies. The fingernail's blessing. I want
you to touch me,
and I want your touch
to be this praise.

I want to listen to you
the way Moses received
God's word for forty days:
full of fear and awe.

And when I awake, I want to destroy
the hands that refuse this music.

~

The Bakers

The bakers below us
pound dough on
tin plates,
abandon them
to wood ovens
after we come.

Our considerate neighbours.

~

Day of Rest

We never leave the bed
except to fill glasses with water.

In the garden, our voices
climb brick walls
braided chicken wire
                    paint
gold and green stars.

In the bedroom, the cat
plays with the head of a mouse,
kicks its ears between the posts of the bed.

Snow beats against the window,
and we wonder if it thinks, cares
or has no worries.

~

Havdalah (end of Sabbath prayer)

This morning
fast asleep in your arms
just before the candles
blew themselves out

I swore to never
speak again
I was drumming
like your breath.

And to smell the spice box
is to hear the night street
tinted windows of taxis
Marxists in the Market.

Shabbos ends, the veil
removed. In the bar:
flat beer, pretzel chatter.
A country band that sings to no one.

Night crawls inside itself.
As though darkness could be touched.

~

Love is not a word
        nor a god

Love is two eyes
        and all that
blue humanness
        staring back at you

IV

BUILDING

Catacomb

Nobody knows where the iron steps lead.
In a Montmartre full of ugly tourists,
four men with head lanterns enter
the belly of the city. All they can see is
the imagined end of their breath.

The manhole sealed shut. No cars, no eyes,
no witnesses, no evidence,
no choice but down.
One consumes darkness as though absence
could be eaten, light
a pigment of the imagination.
Step follows step,
once a man, twice a rat,
conscience longing
in the dank sewers of the night.

There is water past the knees. Islands of bones
piled like pyramids. The dead at this hour
soft on gumboots, crumbling
at their feet, a gentle disintegration.

In an abandoned World War II German bunker
heavy-metal boys from the 20th quarter
hair to their knees and shirts stained with sherry
gather around candles and guitars. *Keep walking past.*
Past the discos and pubs of Montmartre
skidding drunk metres above. Past the torture chambers,
and whipping posts, the multitude of shins.

You want to listen to the dead,
but the dead do not weep, long only
to sink deeper into the earth.

The drumming of these bones
a voice, a rope:
they pull you closer,
take you farther,
to wherever, to whomever it may concern.

No Man's Land

There were no laws. Men carried pistols
or lilies. The funeral women
wept, ate hot cheese bread
and followed the body-of-the-day,
casket open to the sun.
The police demanding Lucky
Strike or cash, blow jobs or Nike.
America. We want it all.

Inside the theatre bar, the girl from the North
stood up and sang
Russian karaoke. The security guard
wept for his father, bloated with shrapnel
in a river in Abkahzia.

I took the hand of Ophelia,
and we started to dance.
Her palm against my heart,
my heart inside her palm.

And when electricity failed,
and darkness held us in its bass,
we curled into its body,
our smoke, skin
and the stars high from benzene.

—Tbilisi, Georgia, 2002

April in Belgrade

When the power goes out, he can see his city of sirens, the bombs'
lightning, dandelions drunk from rain. Even shadows

jab, punch-drunk and broken. 'Did my friends

call from Switzerland or Macedonia?' Jacko asks. He pours clay
coffee, his lichen-lit hands, a verdant electricity. Baba sits,

quiet as stone, too old to walk

the half block to the shelter. On the street below, a fishmonger
trolls to himself, hauls his

right arm in a bag of bloody ice, tentacled

sinew swimming. Bridges show their black teeth and the
water tower talks to itself in flames. Jacko can't remember

the last time faces

slid through his dreams. The voices talking talking. The clay mug
rattles. A toilet sings. What will arrive when the day pulls in?

The Two Thieves of the Desert

Silence unexpected, ties your
hands behind your back and asks the questions: *Who are you?*
And where have you come from? Meanwhile
the desert's hired-gun, Heat,
binds the mouth unaware. Like the victim
of a pickpocket in a crowded bus,
you notice only once it's too late.

Silence and Heat: two thieves of the desert.
Keep you hostage for hours or days.
Patience their sharpest weapon.

Your thoughts ring from Heat.
You're desert drunk, say the Bedouin,
sun-smashed the way a
hangover wobbles a man,
vessel lost at sea.

Accede, says the sun. Leave your vomit or prayers
before the high rock. Give whatever
you have eaten or thought
to the sand.

The colour of Silence the same colour as Sinai:
stone-red and aching.
And feet leave their mark
in the manner of bees and acacia:
invisible, miraculous.

Happiness

There we were: dawn-smashed
bodies, city-sun assaulted,
our skin red and pink
bright like newborn grapefruit.

That's how it is: one minute you're asking a stranger
to pass the dip, the next
you're in a bedroom
squirming until dawn. Fingernails,
thorns, arrows. Uttering the holy
requests: *Will you do this?*
Can you move over to the left? Would you
enter me, please?

For moments the mind stuttered into silence.
And the spiral of pleasure that equals pi:
endless, precise, incalculable.

Was it unfortunate that I was suddenly reminded of
an article in yesterday's paper? *Europe's excessive*
fishing has made the Africans starve
and go inland for meat. The headline in my head
stared at me, thrown
by some invisible paperboy
words rolling to my doorstep
in half-sleep.

Africa starved amidst all of our pleasure.
Europe, gluttonous during the skin's forgetting.

Happiness clung to the wings of the sun.

The Ghost of Trotsky Reminisces Mexico City
For and after Frieda

                              I fucked you
again and over again. While your husband
drank himself Aztec
and my wife tried to forget our country,
our language, I fucked you.
Believed in you,
your people, the howling
of your maimed cunt.

If man is to rise from the ashes
he must learn to cling
to the backside of a good woman.
Must let go of his sloppy thoughts
grab hold of the earth, pigment and pain.

Before the ice pick I hadn't thought of you properly.
But when the spike lodged itself
into the millimetres of skull, when my
grey thoughts
sprang out and sang . . .

I saw your painting in a new light.
Saw myself, stuck in your left eye.

Ferdinand Cheval: Scenes from a Peasant's Temple

In 1879, Ferdinand Cheval, a postman in southern France, began what would become a thirty-three-year project. He collected eight to twenty kilos of stones daily so that he could build his own 'Palace' out of materials he found along his postal route. Though uninhabitable, the Palace remains a remarkable fusion of art forms from both East and West.

'Son of a peasant, it is as a peasant that I wish to live and die
in order to prove that in my class too there are men of energy and genius.'

'Nature wants to make sculpture . . .
I will make the masonry for it.'
                                        —Ferdinand Cheval

Origins: Algeria, 1859

We pulled lumber and spices from the earth.
The wealth sailed to France,
became someone else's
foie gras, electricity, Eiffel Tower.

For six months I laboured between desert and sea.
And though sun and whip
stung me, my back grew strong,
hope bronzed
North African sand.

In a small port I received the gift—
Scientific American, 1859. New Guinea. Galapagos.
Words stained with the world.
And while the others, drunk on Pernod,
cursed the waiting and the ships,
I studied Darwin, listened for his laws.

So says the sea:
any man can build.

If he endures.

~

Stones

In the south of France
I become *un facteur,*
haul the region's mail in *maman*'s thatched basket
thirty-two kilometres daily
de Hauterives à Tersanne.

Road of lupine and ice
sediment and memory
here the sea once stumbled fierce.

Now the clouds
tremble with possibility,
taunt a postman to dream.

For ten years
I follow the clouds' logic
liquid marble
chisel of thunder.

Gardens, grottoes,
towers, statues
I long for
my museum, my castle.

Still the earth rules me.
I fall on a stone,
my right foot almost breaking.

Now rock in hand
creation stares
bold from the minerals

Now limestone speaks
wind listens

God-song
singes my left hand

~

Building

It's like this: one day the land calls you forward
and you find yourself reaching reluctantly
into the fecund cunt of things
et voilà: the world is yours
the way it was when you were born.

The next day I return to the spot. Find tufa, the face of a cougar.
In sandstone the ear of an antelope. A boulder,
David's left thigh. Animals, gods
revealed in the earth.

I haul an extra basket. For thirty-three years
I lift only the beautiful, the talkative, the cursed—
any stone that demands intention.
Carry the rocks to the place I fell.

Boulders become garrets, pebbles
sculptures. Nights alive
with my wheelbarrow and smell.

So the temple builds itself.
And I, peasant,
pay heed to what at night
to me it sings.

~

Commandments

here you must

find	a fossilized snake
	a goblet nestled in earth
unearth	an elm tree
build	the wild Arabian mosque
	otter in sandstone
carve	a lighthouse
	three friends, huddled in coral
	a leopard, larger than lighthouse
construct	the tree of life from seashells
blow	sand
kill	the sun
recite	a psalm

until you turn to dust

~

Statue of My Family

And from a nail hangs the goat
skinned by Father
with his father's
pocket knife, needle-perfect,
the body's curtain removed.

Mother nurses the goat's intestines.

Son plays
with the cat, rubs its nose
against his own.

Singing

love me,
love me
love me

~

Insomnia

See my head on Shiva's limp phallus, his seven arms (marble and onyx)—a work in progress. Above me, a belt of stars tightens midnight, black in the face.

In moonless light, my stonework is no longer me. There's threat in a statue's eyes. The not-knowing in his hands. What might emerge when I'm asleep. Fear of being strangled by my own work.

I need to reacquaint myself, resist the stone's indifference. Need to make peace with what I do.

Forget sleep. The world demands everything. No field where seeds do not seek heaven. No trees, no skies that do not hurl anticipation or demands.

I blow on the fire's embers. When smoke recedes, the smell of jasmine and lavender. In the morning, I will rise and walk to the hill: flowers to gather for my wife, who waits for me in bed.

~

Dear God

The body will not lift.
And the mind declawed
calm now,
        calm.

Today I carry a flask of wine,
cheese, wrapped in a page of Baudelaire:
I am happy where I am not.

Were you watching my knife when it slipped
deep into my left thumb?
A clover of me
stem from stone.

And even though my blood (too quickly)
receded into minerals
I swear the earth
was stained with a smile.

A garden romance, complete.

~

Where I failed

But the wind has not preserved
my faces as it promised.
The tourists thieve pictures,
make postcards of my faith.
There was neglect.
There was no one
to ask for help.

And when I died
no one buried me
where I asked.

Jerusalem of White

The children laughed the way they ought: as though the cold were
ketamine, mainlined to the laughing organ. The soldiers the first
victims, guns stuffed with ice. They were on the lookout for suspi-
cious snowmen, though a few tossed the odd snowball, amazed at
the mark left on sidewalks by exploding snow. One Jew at the Wall
(he hadn't eaten since Jersey) saw a thousand Messiahs swirl before
him, thinking all the scrolled notes, all the handwritten prayers now
fell at once. *Blessed is the white manna of our thoughts that cools us.*

At Ibrahim's coffee shop, the men wept, thinking of their mothers
trapped in Bethlehem, the women who might keep them warm. Or
buried the day's news with coffee, cardamon, shisha. Ibrahim himself
secretly relieved. In the corner near the back, he painted an icicle to
the bruise below his left eye. A psalm of mending.

The Dome of the Rock no longer seemed insistent. It too slept.
While the Church of the Holy Sepulchre still marked the return of
Christ—imminent, but not too imminent. And though King David's
tower endured, wiser, with a thicker beard, a Hasidic boy and a
Muslim girl lost their mothers, their addresses buried beneath ice.
They did what one does, we supposed: they wandered into an alley,
put their hands to the snow, and started to build.

Bus Ride from Cappadocia to Istanbul

i

He is talking to ghosts in the caves.
Christian zealots from the fourth
century, frescoes
alive with their faith. These paintings
reveal something he does not have:
belief, an art
to imagine God.

He wants that life: a truth so great
he must surrender to darkness.
Paint, blindfolded by smell.
He wants narrow stone ladders,
rickety ascension, virgin
cliffs. No food but
the absence of light. And the gift
his body to a god
no one yet knows, to a Christ
before Constantine.

Vision in the Dark Crystal Cathedral.
A verdigris twilight.
Green scarf, green eyes, the gold setting sun.

Alone for days, not sure what's real
in the Valley of the Chimneys.
Believes he sees
the hoarse laughter of friends.
Believes he can hear her smile.

ii

On the bus two days later, the woman with the green scarf
sits beside him. Talk stutters, stops, restarts.
For a moment they've known each other,
ancient hills, shadows joined
in the valley. Gestures
familiar. Until human again, stepping
into silence, stuttering at their
awkward feet.

When they change buses in Nevshihir, they're made to sit
far away from each other, she at the front,
he at the back. *In Turkey*
they prefer, she says, *for the unmarried*
not to sit beside each other.

They drive into darkness. The moon silvers
the forty-five faces of the bus, transforms the black
burkas to milk, liquid crucifixes.
He writes her a letter, passes it forward,
someone tucks it under her sleeping arm.

Do you prefer
To be blind or deaf?
When you dream
What colours do you hear?
When you are bent by the river
Do you see its song?

iii

Call it kismet. Desire, some say.

The American woman one row behind him
falls sick to her stomach, wants to sit at the front.

He suggests she switch with Scarf Woman.
He is one of the rug merchants, generous, for a price.
The haggling comes easy:
Can the Kurd next to me trade
with the Turk next to you?

Deal done. An American for a Turk for a Kurd.
On the bus, the borders are fluid.
The immigrants' demands are few.
And the desire—

geothermal.

iv

A blanket spread over them
receives the full moon

Her breast, slow as a nineteenth-century locomotive
migrates toward his hand

His hand reacts, acts
all aboard, hobo-on-the-jump

Isn't sure if it's familiar or
desire, that big blushing
heart or
the treasure of Cappadocia

They wear the blanket like a shield
the first kiss awkward falling
hands on cold pavement

Have you been to the birthplace of Rumi?
she asks
No, he inscribes in the window
Speak to me in Arabic
he says
Sing to me in Hebrew
she smiles
and they kiss, warm
now, the language
Mohammed and Moses
conjugated

In their minds they lay jasmine
petals by the feet of passengers
When the conductor comes
their kisses have cheated into sleep

Asked for their hands
sprayed with lemon cologne
they dream their train
a gash in a field of sunflowers

Cattle cars
sealed until Istanbul

v

meanwhile, outside
yaweh and allah
recline in the sky
smile, laugh
finish their game of cards

vi

In Istanbul she skips her art class
climbs through the sky into his hotel
surprises him, bored with TV

They watch old Turkish Westerns together
Men die, passionate on the screen
Bullet in the heart, in the head
Death dance, death rattle

Close-up on cactus
sharp and empty
full of its juice
                justice
pusssh . . .

They kiss some
take off their shirts some more
but when he moves to her Levi's
she says *no no no*
This
is forbidden

(gut-shot
blood
a snake bite)

And so he
takes off his pants

Shows her the weapon
between his legs

No more sinister
than a cat, a pen

No more threat
than a pop bottle, a fountain

Quiet   still
& ready

vii

Like the Turkish cowboys on TV she fears
The Final Showdown, but faces it, fearless.
She watches his life
pulled from him. Terrified
by a man's orgasm, worries
she might be electrocuted too. Guilty as charged.

Afterward, in the city, they follow
the back alleys, truckloads of shoes,
billions of shoes for the feet of Asia.
Blocks of fish, pyramids of ice. Mosques by the water,
fire-breathers to the right.
She will not hold his hand in public
but under the bridge she pushes him
against the wall. *Stick 'em up,*
she says. Ready for another duel.

Her parents call, wonder where she is. Still,
she has the right mind to shake his hand, say
thank you, and *good night*.
As though this were a class in etiquette
and the exam, at last, complete.

They descend to the Bosphorus
her green scarf
green eyes
Russian cargo ships
charcoal the coast.

Bold
he thinks she says when she walks away.
I must be bold.

He walks on a street
without lights. The call to prayer
announces the great will of the divine
on loudspeakers, volume turned
past capacity. Feedback
drifts invisible, night-clouds
lie prostrate, devout.

The Bosphorus trembles.
With the smell of her skin.

Notes & Acknowledgements

Below are translations of some words appearing in the text:

Shesh besh is Arabic and Hebrew for backgammon.
Shoichet is Yiddish for ritual slaughterer.
A *minyan* is the quorum for synagogue; ten men are needed to pray.
To *daven* is to pray. *Truah* literally means 'shout' and also refers to the blows on the ram's horn (shofar). The *Beemah* is the raised area in a synagogue that functions as a stage. The *Minsk*, or *Minsker* is a synagogue in Kensington Market, Toronto, built circa 1930. May its beauty be preserved.
A *mezzuzah* is placed on the archways of Jewish homes, inside of which is scrolled the *shma*, the holiest prayer in Judaism.

The line "Is this what you wanted/ to live in a house that is haunted" appears with permission from Leonard Cohen.
The form of "Manitoulin Ferry" is inspired by Robert Kroetsch's *Sad Phoenician*.
"Ferdinand Cheval" is inspired by John Berger's essay, "The Ideal Palace" (*Keeping a Rendezvous*, 1991). Some of the objects in "Commandments" and "Statue of My Family" are drawn from Berger's observations.
The epigraph "Psalm" is translated by Harold Schimmel. "We Travel Like All People" is translated by Munir Akash and Carolyn Forché. "By the Seashore" is translated by D.M. Thomas.
Several of these poems appeared in *CV/2, Descant, Event, Writual, The Shore, Parchment* and *Echolocation*. Thanks to the editors of these journals.

Thanks to:
Ray Bird and Joan Little—their farm and wine to start this.
Bobby Theodore—for the place on rue Clark to 'finish' it.
The Toronto Arts Council for buying me time in-between.
My family for their enduring love, patience and support.

"Mazra' eh al shrqya, West Bank" is for Samer Shalabi. "Qalandya" is for Anne-Marie Filliaire. "Alone in a Room: a Still Life" is for Adam Zagajewski. "Catacomb" is for Forest and Sigrid.

I am very grateful to all who have read this at various stages, providing invaluable commentary, encouragement and guidance, especially Adam Sol, E.C. Woodley, George Elliott Clarke, Paul Thompson and the workshop gang at U of T. Thanks to Dennis Cooley and the Sage Hillers for seeing this at its beginning. And to Dennis, for following through at the end.